ACTION SCIENCE

FLOWERING PLANTS

Alfred Leutscher

Series consultant: Joyce Pope

Franklin Watts

London   New York   Toronto   Sydney

© 1984 Franklin Watts Ltd

First published in Great
Britain in 1984
by Franklin Watts Ltd
12a Golden Square
London W1

First published in the United
States of America by
Franklin Watts Inc.
387 Park Avenue South
New York
N.Y. 10016

Phototypeset by Tradespools
Ltd, Frome, Somerset
Printed in Italy

UK edition:
ISBN 0 86313 186 7
US edition:
ISBN 0-531-03814-9
Library of Congress
Catalog Card Number:
84-51178

Designed by
Ben White

Illustrated by
Colin Newman, Val Sangster/
Linden Artists, and Chris
Forsey

ACTION SCIENCE

FLOWERING PLANTS

Contents

Equipment

As well as a few everyday items, you will need the following equipment to carry out the activities in this book.

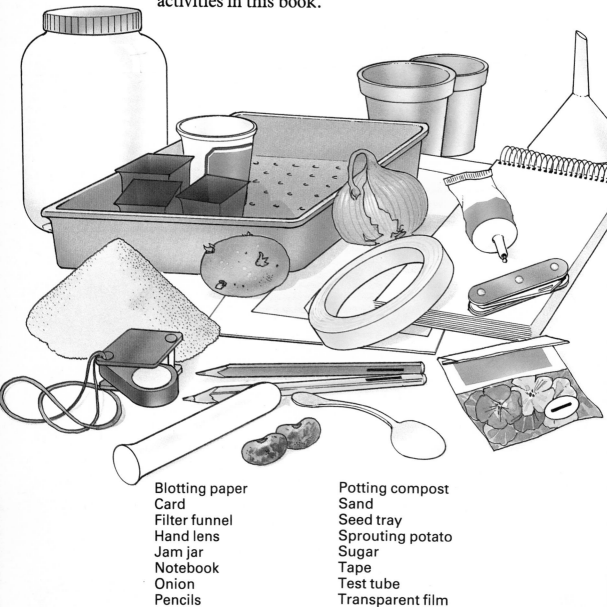

Blotting paper
Card
Filter funnel
Hand lens
Jam jar
Notebook
Onion
Pencils
Plastic pots

Potting compost
Sand
Seed tray
Sprouting potato
Sugar
Tape
Test tube
Transparent film
Old spoon and fork

Introduction

Flowering plants grow almost everywhere—in parks and gardens, woods, meadows, mountains, deserts, seashores, swamps and ponds. Even the smallest place in a corner of a city will not stay bare for long.

Flowering plants cannot grow in darkness, without water, or in very cold surroundings. Few can live in the salty water of the sea. In warm climates, flowers grow all the year round. But in places like Britain and North America where there are seasons, plants produce flowers in spring and summer, and become inactive or die down in winter.

Any plant that produces some sort of flower, however small, is called a flowering plant. The word "flower" can mean the whole plant—the blossom or flower, together with its stem, leaves and roots. More usually, it is used to mean only the blossom.

Flowering plants vary greatly in size from tiny, water-growing duckweeds to trees that may be about 100ft (30m) tall. The largest flower in the world is the tropical Rafflesia, measuring up to 3ft (1m) across. The most noticeable flowers are those that are brightly colored, but many plants, such as grasses and some trees, have green or dull-colored flowers that are easy to overlook.

We depend on flowering plants for our food. They provide grains, fruits and vegetables. Even the animals that we use for food live on flowering plants.

Keeping a record

One of the best ways to find out about flowering plants is to look at the ones growing near where you live. If you do not have a garden, you can visit a park. Or, you can go to a wood or meadow. Even a waste site in a town may have wild flowers growing.

Wherever you go, take a drawing book and make colored sketches and notes of the flowers you see. If you have a camera, try taking photographs as well. It is a good idea to carry a flower guide book to help you identify flowers.

If you see a lot of the same wild flowers growing in one place, pick one and start a collection. Use your guide book to make sure it is a common flower before you pick it.

△Drawing and taking photographs are two ways of keeping a record of the plants you find.

▷When making a color drawing of a flower, include as many details as you can. Show the stem and leaves as well as the flower. If there is an unopened flower bud and an old flower without its colored petals, show these too. Make a note of the date and a short description of the surroundings in which the plant is growing. If you know its name, include this as well. Use a tape measure to find the height of the plant.

A hand lens is useful for studying small details.

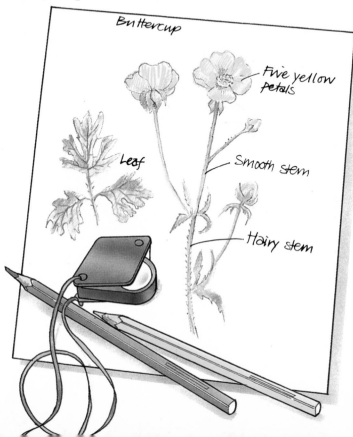

Buttercup

Five yellow petals

Leaf

Smooth stem

Hairy stem

Drying and pressing

Preserving flowers is another way to make a record of what you find. You can add to a collection year by year, as you visit different places. Always make sure you only pick common flowers.

One method is to press and dry the flower and then mount it in a book. The other way is to dry the flower in sand, so that it keeps its shape. Then you can store it in a box lined with cotton. In either case, do not forget to add a note of the name of the flower and the date and place where you found it.

To make your flower notes more interesting, try to find out the origin of the flowers' names. Some names go back as far as ancient Greek mythology. Others, like self-heal, lungwort and speedwell were given to plants used as medicines.

Most museums have collections of pressed flowers called herbariums. Some large museums have herbariums containing millions of plants from all over the world.

heavy books

blotting paper

△To press and dry a flower, lay it between two sheets of blotting paper. Place a pile of books on top and leave it for about a week. When the flower is dried out, fix it in your flower book with small strips of tape.

▷To preserve a flower in its natural shape, you need some aquarium sand, sold in pet shops, and a wood or cardboard box. The sand must be thoroughly dry.

Pour a layer of sand into the box and place your flower on it. Carefully pour on more sand until the flower is covered. Leave it for a few weeks to make sure the flower loses all its moisture, or it will get moldy.

fine sand

7

Parts of a flower

The first thing you will notice when you look at most flowers is the attractive, sweet-smelling petals. Petals are usually large and brightly colored. They may be red, yellow, blue, purple, orange, white, or pink as in the dog rose shown here. The petals are brightly colored and scented to attract insects to the flower.

Below the petals are the sepals. They are usually much smaller than the petals and are green. Their main purpose is to protect the flower from damage. This is particularly important in the young bud stage when the sepals completely enclose all the other parts of the flower.

▽To study the parts of a flower, choose one which has a regular, open shape so that each part can be easily seen. The flower shown here is the dog rose, which grows in hedgerows.

Pick a flower and cut it carefully down the center with a sharp knife so that you can see all the parts. Make a colored drawing and name each part.

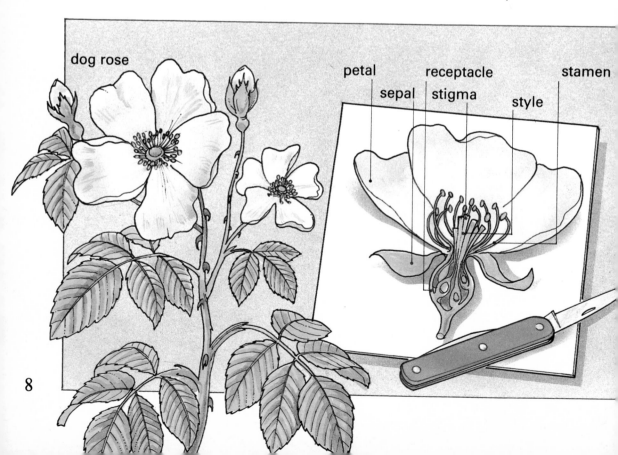

dog rose

petal
sepal
stigma
receptacle
style
stamen

female flower

male flower

△Many trees have flowers that are very small and grow in tight bunches called catkins. The male and female parts are in separate catkins. They hang loosely so that the wind will blow pollen from the male catkins to the female catkins.

Male and female parts

Most flowers have both male and female parts. The male parts are the stamens clustered around the center of the flower. They produce dust-like, sticky grains called pollen. The female parts are the ovaries hidden in the bulbous receptacle at the base of the flower. Each ovary has a stalk called the style, with a swollen tip called the stigma.

The purpose of the whole flower is to produce seeds from which new plants can grow. To do this, pollen must be transferred from the male stamen to the female stigma of an ovary. Then the ovules inside the ovaries grow to become seeds. The ovaries and receptacle swell to protect the developing seeds. The swollen parts are known as fruits. In the dog rose they are called hips.

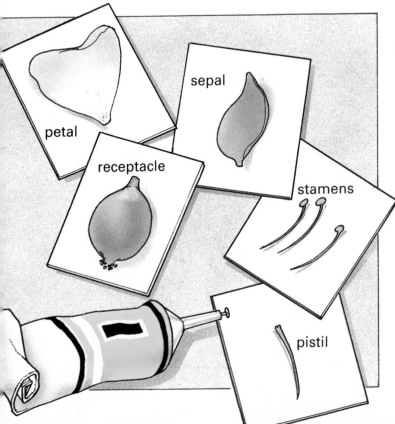

petal

sepal

receptacle

stamens

pistil

◁Pick a dog rose, or similar flower, in full flower. You should be able to see both the male stamens and the female stigmas in the center of the petals.

Carefully separate all the parts of the flower and select one of each. You should find a petal, a sepal, a style with its stigma (together called the pistil), a stamen and the receptacle. Use a sharp knife to cut the receptacle down the middle to show the ovaries.

Take five pieces of white card and glue one part to each. Label each one and then cover it with transparent film.

Flower families

Flowering plants are divided into families according to the shape of the flowers and the number of parts they have. Some examples of flowers belonging to different families are shown below.

In the Buttercup family, called the *Ranunculaceae*, the flowers have regular, open shapes, and many stamens. The fruits are a collection of nutlets, called achenes.

In the family called *Compositae*, what looks like a single flower is really a collection of tiny flowers, bunched together. The flowers produce many seeds and spread into many places. Some flowers from this family, such as the dandelion and daisy, are treated as weeds in gardens.

anemone

dandelion

sweet pea

△Anemones belong to the Buttercup family. This one is the wild wood anemone, also called the windflower because it trembles in the wind.

△The dandelion is a well-known member of the *Compositae* family. It spreads rapidly because its parachute seeds are carried by the wind.

△The sweet pea is popular because of its color and scent. It is a member of the *Leguminosae* and can climb up to about 6ft (2m) tall.

Members of the *Leguminosae* have flowers with five petals arranged in a special way. The upper one, shaped like a hood, is called the standard. The two side petals are called wings. The two lower ones are joined together in a boatlike shape called the keel. The fruit is a pod that contains the seeds.

The Rose family, *Rosaceae*, has flowers with sepals and petals arranged in fives. They have many stamens. Members of this family often have an extra circle of sepals.

Flowers of the *Umbelliferae* family are mostly small and colored white. They form at the ends of stems which are joined at one end and spread out like the ribs of an umbrella.

The Wallflower belongs to the *Cruciferae* family (meaning a cross). The four petals form the shape of a cross.

apple

cow parsley

wallflower

△All varieties of apple belong to the *Rosaceae*. Other fruit trees such as the pear and cherry also belong to this family. They are covered with blossom in spring.

△Cow parsley is one of the first of the *Umbelliferae* family to bloom in the hedgerow. It has umbrella-like flower stalks which give the family its name.

△The wallflower is a member of the *Cruciferae*. It is an upright, bushy plant and is popular as a garden flower. It blooms in late spring.

Pollination

If you look at flowers in full bloom on a sunny summer day, you will see many different insects visiting one flower after another. The bright colors and scent attract them but they are really looking for a sweet, sugary liquid called nectar, or pollen, which some of them use as a food.

When an insect visits a flower, sticky pollen grains from the male stamens get caught in the hairs on its body. These grains may rub off onto the female stigmas of the next flower it visits. Many plants depend on insects to carry pollen in this way from the stamens of one flower to the stigmas of another. This process is called pollination. It is an important part of the reproductive cycle.

Some flowers, such as those of grasses and the catkins of some trees are not colorful and have no scent. Because of this, they do not attract insects. They produce dry pollen which is carried by the wind.

△The dull-colored rye grass and the plantain above are pollinated by the wind, but all the other flowers rely on insects to pollinate them.

Insect visitors

The insects which you are most likely to see visiting flowers for their nectar are bees, wasps, butterflies, hoverflies and some day-flying moths. Among the flowers they find most attractive are buddleia (also called the butterfly bush), petunia, golden rod, ice plant and wild aster.

Some flowers, such as night-scented stock, tobacco plant and honeysuckle are pale colored and most strongly scented at night. They have developed to attract large moths, such as the hawkmoths, which are night flyers.

If you examine different flower petals you will see that some have colored stripes or dotted lines. These are called honey guides and help to lead insects toward the nectar.

▽ Cut four simple flower shapes from white cardboard. Color one pink with red honey guides (A). Do the same with (B) but add a blob of honey in the center. Leave (C) white and add a honey blob. Leave (D) white, but draw on black honey guides and do not add honey.

Fix the flowers to stakes and support them in jam jars. Place them outside near some garden flowers.

Because flower (B) has scent, color and honey it will probably attract the most insects.

honey guides

Flower shapes

The shape of a flower also plays an important part in the process of pollination. Flowers that rely on insect pollination must be visited by insects carrying pollen from other flowers of the same kind or species. Only male and female parts of the same species can fuse and give rise to seeds which grow into new plants.

Flowers with a flat, open shape, such as wild asters and sunflowers, are visited by hoverflies and several kinds of bees. Others, such as wallflowers and nasturtiums that have the lower part of their petals fused into a tube, attract insects with long tongues. They can reach down the petal tube to the nectar. Honeysuckle has long narrow petal tubes. Hawkmoths hover in front of the flowers while their long tongues reach inside to find the nectar.

Flowers belonging to the pea family have petals that enclose the male and female parts. They can only be opened by heavy insects such as bumble bees. Members of this family include lupines and sweet peas.

sweet pea

keel pushed down

pollen

wing petals cut away

▷Watch a bee as it settles on a lupin or sweet pea flower. It lands on the two lower petals, pushing aside the two wing petals as it does so. As the bee reaches inside to suck nectar, the underside of its body brushes against the stamens and is dusted with pollen. This is carried to the next flower, where some of the pollen brushes onto the stigma.

14

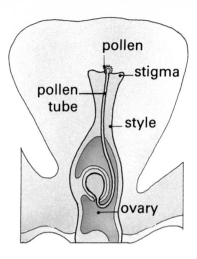

pollen

stigma

pollen tube

style

ovary

▽This experiment shows the growth of pollen tubes. Pour some warm water into a saucer and add plenty of sugar. Allow the mixture to dissolve, then sprinkle on pollen from different flowers—ripe grasses, clover and ragwort, for example. Cover the saucer to keep out dust.

In a day or so, using a hand lens, you should be able to see some pollen tubes.

Fertilization

After pollination, the contents of the male pollen grains must fuse with the contents of the female ovules. Then seeds begin to form. This process is called fertilization.

As soon as a pollen grain lands on a stigma, a thin tube starts to grow from it. It grows down the style to the ovary and then through the ovary wall to the ovule inside. When the tip of the tube touches the ovule it dissolves. The contents pass into the ovule and fertilization occurs.

Some flowers can use their own pollen for fertilization. In time, this may weaken the species. To prevent self-fertilization, most flowers stop producing pollen before their stigmas are fully developed.

saucer covered with sheet of glass

mixture of pollen grains

sugar solution

15

Seed dispersal

Seeds would not have enough light, water or food to grow if they simply fell to the ground around their parent plant. So plants have developed ways of scattering their seeds. This is known as seed dispersal.

The tiny seeds of grasses and hanging catkins are light enough to be carried by the wind. Some larger seeds also rely on the wind or air currents, but they have aids to help them. For example, sycamore seeds have wings and dandelions have hairy parachutes.

Animals and birds also help to disperse seeds. Seeds with hooks get caught on animal fur and our clothes. Birds feed on soft fruits and the seeds inside pass through their bodies unharmed.

Some plants have special explosive mechanisms for seed dispersal.

△Birds, such as starlings, feed on fallen apple fruits. They digest the soft fruit but the seeds inside go through their bodies unharmed, passing out in their droppings.

△The fruit of Herb Robert is a long capsule. When the seeds inside it are ripe and the fruit is dry and brittle, it bursts open, throwing the seeds out as it does so.

△The dandelion flower head develops into a mass of seeds, each with a hairy parachute. You can disperse the seeds by blowing on the flower head.

△Squirrels often bury acorns in store for winter and forget where they have hidden them. If this happens, the seeds inside grow into trees.

16

Taking over waste places

Wherever there is a neglected corner of land plants will start to grow. If you live in a town look for derelict sites and waste places, often near factories and car parks. Study the flowering plants in these places to try to find out how their seeds are dispersed. Count how many of each kind you see. The ones which there are most of are likely to have the most efficient ways of spreading and surviving in poor conditions.

The first flowering plants to grow in a waste place are usually those with tiny seeds carried by wind, such as fireweed, dandelions and grasses. After these come seeds dispersed by birds and then seeds that are carried by animals.

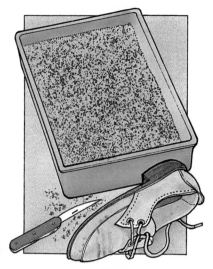

△Try scraping mud off your shoes after a walk. Put the mud onto a tray filled with compost. You may be surprised to see plants start to grow!

▷Look at waste ground near your home and see which flowers grow there.

▽To study seed dispersal, place a tray of potting compost outdoors in an open position in summer. Watch for several weeks to see what grows.

How seeds grow

When seeds settle on the ground they may start to grow or "germinate" into new plants straight away. But often there is a period of rest until spring, when the soil becomes warm and damp enough for the seeds to swell and germinate. Seeds also need oxygen from the air to allow them to breathe.

First the root develops and grows down into the soil. The root has tiny hairs which take in water. Then the shoot, which will bear leaves and flowers, starts to grow and appears above the ground.

▽ To grow your own seeds, fill a seed tray with potting compost. Scatter some seeds thinly on it and cover with another layer of compost. Pat this down gently and water lightly.

As the plants start to grow, use an old spoon to dig the strongest ones out. Put these into pots filled with compost.

sprinkle seed   cover with compost   seedlings

seed   old spoon

fiber pots

clay pots

From seed to plant

When seeds first start to germinate they use the food stored in their seed leaves or "cotyledons." In many plants the cotyledons are pushed above ground as the shoot starts to develop. They turn green and look like ordinary leaves. The cotyledons continue to provide food for the growing plant until the shoot develops proper leaves which can make food. The young roots take water and minerals from the soil.

Some plants grow and produce flowers and seeds more quickly than others. Flowering plants such as marigolds are called annuals. The seeds germinate and grow into plants which flower and produce more seeds all in the same year. A biennial, such as a foxglove, takes two years for this growth cycle. In the first year the seeds germinate and grow into plants, and in the second year the plants flower and produce seeds. Perennials live for many years, flowering each year.

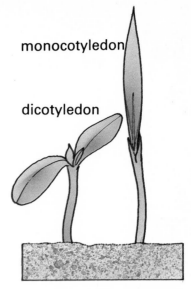

monocotyledon

dicotyledon

△ The seeds of most flowering plants have two seed leaves or cotyledons. These plants are called dicotyledons. They always have broad-shaped leaves.

Some seeds have only a single seed leaf. These are called monocotyledons. They have narrow leaves.

◁ As your seedlings grow larger you should replant them. If you do not have a garden, transfer them to larger pots with a mixture of compost and soil. Place a few stones or pieces of old clay pot in the bottom of each plant pot. This prevents the soil becoming too wet.

To plant your seedlings in a garden, first remove any large stones or weeds from the soil. Make holes with your finger or a stick and carefully put a seedling in each hole.

19

Plant survival

no minerals

no water

no light

Unlike animals, plants can make their own food. Leaves contain a green substance called chlorophyll. Chlorophyll uses sunlight to make energy. This energy enables the plant to make food from carbon dioxide in the air and water. This process is called photosynthesis.

So, in order to make food, plants need sunlight, carbon dioxide and water. They also need minerals from the soil for growth. Water containing minerals is absorbed from the soil by tiny hairs on the root tips. It is then drawn up through the stems to the leaves. Water also keeps most plants upright and rigid. Without water they wilt and die.

In the experiment on this page, you will find that only the control plant looks healthy after a week or so. The plant in sand does not grow because there are no minerals in sand. The plant without water wilts and dies. The plant in the dark cannot make food so it loses its chlorophyll and becomes pale and spindly in its search for light.

△Take four plants. Put one in a pot of sand in a sunny place and water it. Put the others in pots of soil. The first should be left in a sunny place without water and the second in a dark place with water. The third is used as a control and given both water and a sunny place. Leave the pots for a few days and see what happens.

20

An oxygen supply

Plant leaves have minute holes or pores on their surfaces. These are too small to see with your naked eye. Most of the pores are under the leaf. Carbon dioxide is drawn in through them during photosynthesis.

Oxygen is produced as a waste product of photosynthesis and leaves the plant through the leaf pores. This is one reason why plants are so valuable to us. They use up carbon dioxide which we breathe out and give us new supplies of oxygen to breathe in.

Water also passes through the leaf pores. It is moving up through the plant to the leaves all the time and is released as vapor after being used in photosynthesis.

▽ Stand a leafy pot plant such as a geranium in a sunny position. Carefully place a clear plastic bag over one leaf and tape it around the leaf stalk. After a few hours, you will see moisture inside the bag.

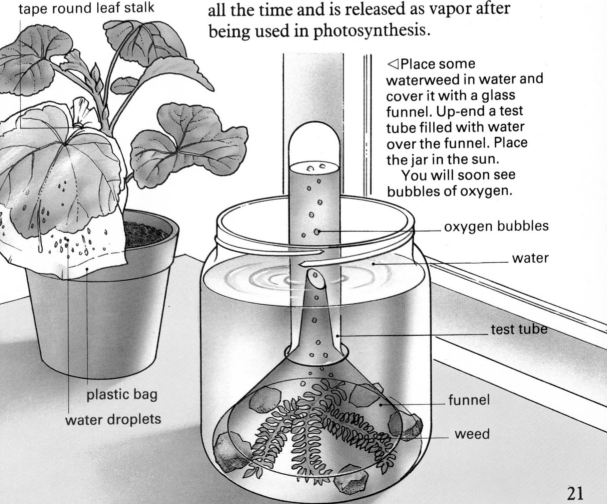

tape round leaf stalk

plastic bag

water droplets

◁Place some waterweed in water and cover it with a glass funnel. Up-end a test tube filled with water over the funnel. Place the jar in the sun.
You will soon see bubbles of oxygen.

oxygen bubbles

water

test tube

funnel

weed

Storing food

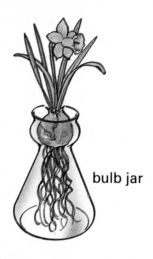

bulb jar

△ Bulbs such as tulips, hyacinths and daffodils can be grown in a special bulb jar.

Flowering plants make food so that they can grow and develop. Plants that are annuals only make as much food as they need to produce seeds, and then they die. A small amount of food is stored in the seed cotyledons to enable the seeds to germinate.

Plants that live for more than one year need to store food over the winter so that they are ready to grow again as soon as the weather gets warmer in spring. Some of these plants die down above ground but store food below the ground in special storage organs, such as bulbs, or in swollen roots.

A single bulb may contain more than one bud that can grow into a new plant.

next year's leaves

brown, protective leaf

flower bud

fleshy, food-storing leaves

stem

△ The diagram shows an onion cut in half. You can see the bulb's fleshy leaves which protect the central bud and leaves. They also supply food.

Growing plants from storage organs

Because storage organs are below ground they are safe in all weathers. They help a plant to survive during bad conditions such as droughts or very cold weather. The stored food can be used when the plant starts to grow again when the conditions are right for it.

Try cutting off the tops of the swollen roots of a carrot and a parsnip. Place them in shallow dishes containing sandy soil. Pour on a little warm water. Soon you will see tiny roots starting to grow near the cut edge of the storage organs and leaves growing from the top end. The stored food is enough for leaves to develop but not for a flower to grow.

You can also try growing a potato plant. Potatoes are tubers, that is, the swollen, food-storing tips of special underground stems called rhizomes.

▽ Choose a potato with plenty of "eyes" or buds and leave them to sprout. When several buds have sprouted, select the two strongest and rub the rest off with your fingers.

Place some stones in the bottom of a bucket for drainage, then half fill it with soil. Plant the potato with the buds upward so they appear just above the soil.

parsnip

carrot

sprouting "eyes"

23

Plant movements

Although a plant stays anchored by its roots in one place, the different parts of it can show some movement. These movements are known as "tropisms." They are caused by the plant's response to light, water and gravity (the downward pull that exists on Earth).

Because light is needed for photosynthesis, a plant's shoot normally grows upward toward the sun. This is called phototropism.

Try the maze experiment to show that a shoot grows toward light. Sprout a string bean seed in a small jar and place it in one end of a shoe box. Fix a few partitions across the box as shown, then put on the lid. The bean shoot should find its way through the maze and its tip will grow out of the opening.

▽Line a glass jar with damp blotting paper and put some bean seeds at different angles between the paper and the jar. No matter which way the beans are placed, the shoots grow upward toward light and the roots grow downward in response to gravity.

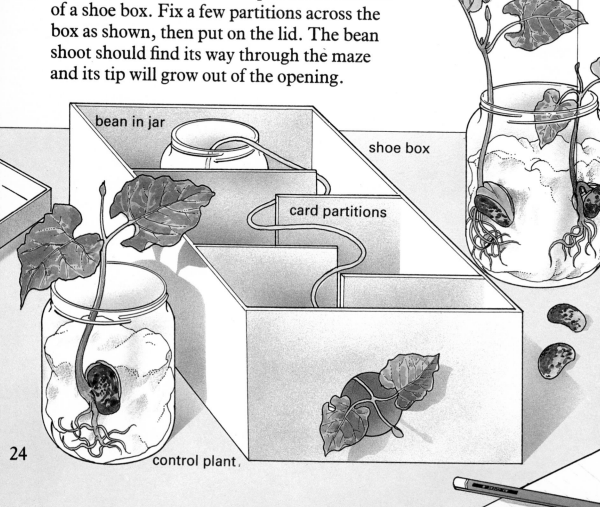

bean planted upside down

bean in jar

shoe box

card partitions

control plant

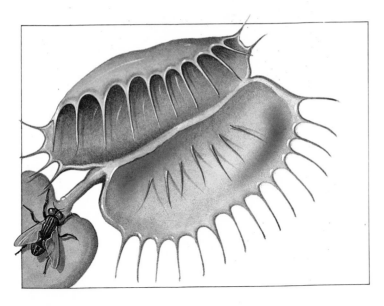

◁The Venus flytrap plant gets food from insects, as well as making its own food by photosynthesis. Hinged lobes at the end of its leaves have sensitive hairs. These act like triggers. When an insect lands on these, the lobes snap shut and trap the insect inside. The leaf hairs then produce a substance to digest the insect. The Venus flytrap usually grows in damp bogs.

▽Line a glass jar with blotting paper and put a string bean seed between the paper and the jar. Keep it watered. When the bean has grown a shoot, place the jar on its side. The shoot will bend upward.

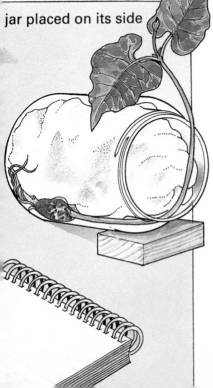

jar placed on its side

Touch and temperature movements

In addition to the movements called tropisms, a few plants will respond to being touched. The mimosa, or sensitive plant, is a good example of this. Its leaves are composed of a number of small leaflets. When these are touched, they immediately fold up together and the whole leaf appears to droop. The movement is due to a sudden loss of water at the base of the leaf stalk. When the plant tissue in the stalk takes in more water, it becomes rigid again and the leaf rises to its normal position.

In some plants, such as daisies, the flowers open in daytime, and close at night and in bad weather. This "sleep movement" prevents rain and dew getting inside the flowers and wetting the pollen. If the flowers have to stay closed for several days, they will fertilize themselves.

Other flowers, such as the crocus, are affected by temperature. The flower opens up its petals as the day warms up. On days when there is no sun they stay closed.

Different habitats

The place where a plant grows is called its habitat. Examples of different habitats are woodland, mountains, deserts, ponds, marshes, roadsides and seashore cliffs. Each habitat has special features, for example, the soil will vary from one habitat to another. It may be clay, chalk, sand or peat. The temperature will also vary from place to place and so will the amount of sunlight and water that the plants get.

Some habitats are very small and are known as micro-habitats. These may be a damp hollow in dry surroundings, or a rotting tree stump or log in a wood. Towns provide a number of different micro-habitats for plants such as cracks in old walls and on patches of waste ground.

△ Choose any patch of ground where plants are growing and mark out an area about 3ft (1m) square. Place sticks at the corners and tie tape around to mark the square.

Study the place you have chosen. Is it in the open or shade? Is the ground wet or dry? Does the soil seem to be light and chalky, is it heavy like clay, or is it in between these extremes?

Make sketches of the plants in your square and use a flower guide book to identify them.

△Woodland plants usually flower in spring. They include the wood anemone, lords and ladies and ivy.

△Few plants grow on acid soils but heathers and some herbs do well. Various grasses also survive well.

△Plants that live by the sea often have special features to help them withstand the poor, salty conditions.

▽Many flowering plants thrive on warm, dry chalky soil.

The features of a habitat determine which flowering plants can grow there. In woodlands, flowers usually grow in spring. This is because in summer the trees are covered with leaves and the ground below is often too shady.

On open, rocky land, where the soil is thin, and lacking in minerals, few plants can grow. Those that do must be able to stand exposed, windy conditions. Many flowering plants grow on chalky hills, mainly because the soil is warm. Because of this, chalklands are good places to visit to find a wide variety of flowers. Plants that grow near the sea can withstand salt in the air and the ground. They need deep roots to anchor them in sand or gravel. Their leaves are often able to store water.

Growing plants

Plants from pits and stones

It is quite easy to grow plants from the pits and stones of fruit you have eaten. But they will probably not produce flowers when grown in pots. Try growing apple, orange and tomato pits and peach stones as shown here.

Making a bottle garden

A bottle garden needs little attention once it is set up in a large glass jar with a lid or cork. The plants give off water vapor during photosynthesis. This forms water droplets on the glass which run back down into the soil and can be taken up again by the plants' roots. As a result, a bottle garden does not need watering.

Set up a soil mixture in the bottle as shown, and gather a selection of plants which grow best in warm, moist conditions. Plants that will do well include African violets, Begonias, the prayer plant, the fig and various kinds of ivy and ferns.

▷To grow pits, first soak them in warm water for a few days. Then plant them in seed compost in plastic pots. Keep the compost moist and put the pots in a warm, dark place to encourage germination. Plant two or three of each kind because not all of them will grow.

▽To grow a peach plant you will need the stone from a very ripe peach. If the stone is still hard after soaking it in warm water, tap it gently with a hammer to make a crack big enough for moisture to get in. Plant in the same way as pits.

peach

tomato

orange

apple

▽To prepare a bottle garden, first pour in a layer of pebbles. Then add a layer of charcoal (from a garden shop), and finish with a layer of compost. Use an old spoon tied to a stick to make holes in the compost for the plants. Then use this spoon and a fork tied to a cane to lower the plants gently down into the holes. Firm the soil around each plant. Use a water sprayer to dampen the compost and put the lid on the bottle.

long-handled fork

water sprayer

compost

charcoal

pebbles

29

Glossary

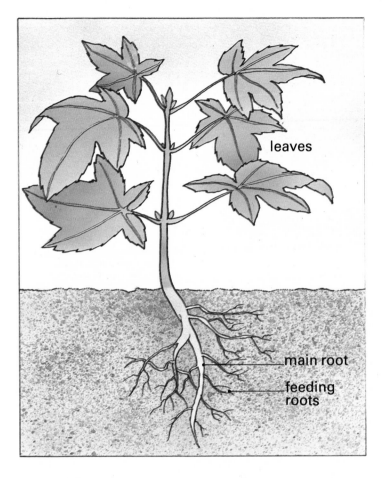

leaves

main root

feeding roots

Anther
The part of a stamen which contains the pollen grains.

Catkin
A tight bunch of small flowers, either male or female.

Chlorophyll
The green chemical in plants used for making food.

Cotyledon
The seed-leaf of a flowering plant. Some grow one seed leaf (monocotyledon) and others two (dicotyledon).

Embryo
A very young plant before it germinates.

Fertilization
The union of a pollen grain with the egg-cell inside the ovary.

Geotropism
The downward movement of a plant's roots in response to gravity.

Germination
The sprouting of a seed into a plant.

Habitat
The surroundings in which a plant grows.

Herbarium
A collection of preserved plants.

Honey guides
The markings on a flower's petals, usually in lines. They guide insects toward the nectar inside the flowers.

Hydrotropism
The movement of a plant's roots towards water.

△Each part of a plant has an important job. The roots anchor the plant in the ground and take up water from the soil. The stem carries water to the leaves and the leaves make food.

Mineral salts
The chemicals in the soil which are taken up in water by a plant's roots and used as food.

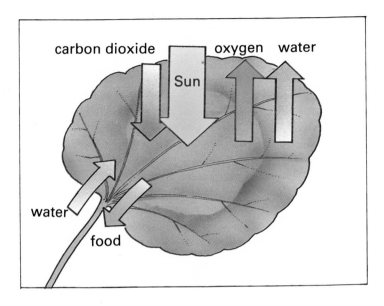

carbon dioxide   oxygen   water

Sun

water

food

◁Water and mineral salts flow through the leaf stalk and into the network of veins all over the leaf. To make food, the leaf must also have a supply of sunlight and carbon dioxide. During the process of food making, known as photosynthesis, oxygen and water vapor are released.

Ovary
The female organ in a flower which contains the egg-cell.

Photosynthesis
A plant's method of making food with the aid of chlorophyll and the energy of sunlight. This occurs mainly in the leaves.

Phototropism
A plant's movement in response to light. This occurs in the leaves and shoots.

Pollination
The transferring of pollen by wind or insect onto the stigma of the ovary.

Stamen
A flower's male organ.

Stigma
The part of a flower's female organ which receives the pollen.

Transpiration
The act of giving off water vapor from the leaves of plants.

Tuber
A plant's storage organ which grows underground.

Index